# Zodiacal Roots

# Zodiacal Roots

## The Astrological Soul of Hemp

Matthew Petchinsky

Apophis Enterprises LLC

Zodiacal Roots: The Astrological Soul of Hemp
By: Matthew Petchinsky

## Introduction 1A

Astrology has been a fascination for thousands of years, there are many different versions of it and it has had the hearts and mind of man in every culture on Earth, since mankind was primitive Caveman in a cave to Egyptian to modern man. Astrology is engrained in our DNA. Please enjoy this book.

Hemp has been used for thousands of years, it is ingrained in our DNA as well. Take a deep look into a mixture of Hemp and Astrology.

## Introduction 2B

In the tapestry of human culture, two ancient threads—astrology and hemp—have been intertwined in a complex and often misunderstood dance. Both astrology and hemp boast histories that stretch back thousands of years, serving myriad purposes in various societies, from the spiritual to the medicinal, the practical to the prophetic. This book, "Zodiacal Roots: The Astrological Soul of Hemp," aims to explore the deep connections between the cosmos as understood through astrology and the versatile plant that is hemp. Our journey is not merely one of historical curiosity but of understanding how the alignment of the stars and planets at the time of our birth can influence our interactions with this ancient plant, particularly in the realm of healing and personal well-being.

Astrology, the study of the movements and relative positions of celestial bodies interpreted as having an influence on human affairs and the natural world, offers a personalized blueprint of an individual's life, character, and preferences. Hemp, on the other hand, is a manifestation of nature's power to heal, comfort, and sustain human life. The plant has been used for centuries in various cultures for its medicinal properties, as well as for making textiles, paper, and even as a food source. The convergence of astrology and hemp represents a fusion of cosmic energy and earth's bounty, suggesting that our personal astrological makeup might influence how we can best utilize hemp in our lives.

Understanding one's astrological roots, therefore, becomes more than an exercise in self-discovery; it becomes a practical guide to living a more harmonious life. For instance, an individual with a predominance of fiery Aries energy might find different uses for hemp than a water-sign Cancer, not just in terms of personal health and wellness, but also in the manner of engaging with hemp's diverse applications. This book seeks to delve into these distinctions, offering insights into how each zodiac sign can best harness the benefits of hemp, from medicinal uses to dietary and environmental practices.

The purpose of "Zodiacal Roots" is twofold. First, it serves as an educational primer on the history and uses of hemp, exploring how this plant has been perceived and employed throughout the ages. This exploration is not merely academic; it is a journey into understanding how our ancestors utilized hemp and how we can draw upon this wisdom in contemporary times. Second, the book aims to establish a unique dialogue between each zodiac sign and hemp. By understanding the astrological implications of our personalities, we can tailor our approach to using hemp, maximizing its benefits in our lives. Whether through medicinal applications, dietary supplements, or eco-friendly lifestyle choices, the symbiosis between our astrological blueprint and hemp can offer a path to greater health and ecological consciousness.

As we embark on this exploration, "Zodiacal Roots" invites readers to open their minds to the ancient wisdom of astrology and the enduring versatility of hemp. Together, we will uncover the astrological soul of hemp, learning how the stars and this remarkable plant can guide us toward a deeper understanding of ourselves and our place in the natural world.

## Chapter 1: The Cosmic Cannabis Connection

In the grand narrative of human history, both astrology and cannabis (specifically, hemp, a non-psychoactive strain of the cannabis plant) have carved their indelible marks on the cultural and spiritual practices of countless civilizations. This chapter delves into the historical and cosmic connection between astrology and hemp, tracing their intertwined paths from ancient times to modern-day interpretations, revealing how the wisdom of the past informs contemporary practices in surprising and profound ways.

### Ancient Alignments: Astrology and Hemp in Antiquity

The story begins under the vast, starlit skies of ancient civilizations, where the mysteries of the cosmos were deeply intertwined with the rhythms of the natural world. Astrology, a practice as old as civilization itself, offered these societies a framework to understand these mysteries, guiding everything from agricultural cycles to royal decrees. Parallel to this celestial guidance, hemp emerged as a versatile and vital crop, revered for its medicinal, nutritional, and fibrous qualities.

Evidence suggests that the ancient Sumerians, Babylonians, and Egyptians, among others, cultivated hemp and held astrology in high esteem, though direct links between their astrological practices and hemp cultivation are more inferential than explicit. However, the significance both held in these cultures suggests a harmonious relationship, with planting and harvesting cycles likely influenced by astrological calendars and celestial events.

In ancient China, the relationship between hemp and astrology becomes more pronounced. The Chinese zodiac, a fundamental aspect of Chinese astrology, is intertwined with agricultural practices and natural medicine—two realms where hemp held a place of honor. The ancient Chinese pharmacopeia, "The Herbal" (Shennong Bencaojing), attributed to the legendary Emperor Shennong, lists hemp seeds among its entries, praising their medicinal properties. This text, and others like it, likely informed agricultural practices aligned with the celestial calendar, suggesting a sophisticated understanding of the interplay between the cosmos and the cultivation of hemp.

**Stellar Symbiosis: The Spiritual and Medicinal Bridge**

As civilizations evolved, so too did their understanding of the stars and the myriad uses of hemp. In many cultures, the stars were not merely lights in the night sky but divine entities or symbols with direct influence over the health and prosperity of the land and its people. This celestial influence extended to the realm of herbal medicine, where the properties of plants, including hemp, were often classified according to astrological principles.

Astrological herbalism, a practice that assigns planetary rulerships to plants based on their medicinal qualities and spiritual significances, provided a framework for using hemp in healing rituals and treatments. For instance, a plant associated with Venus might be used to treat conditions of the heart or to foster harmony and love, while Mars-ruled plants could be applied to ailments requiring a more aggressive approach to healing. Hemp, with its myriad uses, likely found its place within this astrological herbal framework, prescribed according to the planetary influences governing a patient's health concerns.

**From Ancient Roots to Modern Branches: The Revival of Cosmic Cannabis Wisdom**

In the contemporary era, the ancient connections between astrology and hemp are experiencing a renaissance, as modern seekers of wellness and spiritual growth rediscover and reinterpret these traditional wisdoms. Today, the practice of aligning hemp use with astrological principles is being revitalized, offering personalized approaches to health and well-being that echo the ancients' understanding of the cosmos.

Astrological wellness, a holistic approach that integrates the ancient wisdom of astrology with modern lifestyle and health practices, now often includes hemp-derived products. From CBD oils governed by the calming influence of the Moon to hemp seeds energized under the auspicious stars of Venus, individuals are increasingly turning to astrologically informed hemp solutions to balance and harmonize their physical and spiritual selves.

Moreover, the eco-friendly and sustainable qualities of hemp resonate with contemporary astrological movements towards environmental consciousness, reflecting a cosmic mandate to live in harmony with the Earth. Astrology, with its focus on cycles and transitions, mirrors the sustainable cycles of hemp cultivation, highlighting the plant's role in ecological balance and the health of the planet.

**Conclusion: A Celestial Synergy**

The cosmic connection between astrology and hemp is a testament to humanity's enduring quest to understand and harness the energies of the cosmos and the natural world. From the ancient fields of hemp swaying under a starry sky to the modern embrace of astrologically aligned wellness practices, this connection speaks to a deep-seated recognition of the interdependence of all things. As we continue to explore the astrological soul of hemp, we are reminded of the ancient wisdom that guides us toward balance, health, and harmony with the universe.

If you want to see some amazing products, please visit my Virtual Dispensary: https://shift.store/sg1fan23477/retail

## Chapter 2: Astrological Principles and Plant Medicine

In our journey through "Zodiacal Roots: The Astrological Soul of Hemp," we turn now to a foundational understanding that bridges the celestial with the terrestrial: the principles of astrology and their interplay with plant medicine. This chapter lays the groundwork for understanding how the positions of stars and planets at the time of our birth not only influence our personalities and destinies but also how we interact with the natural world, particularly the healing powers of plants.

### The Basics of Astrology

Astrology is a complex system that interprets the influence of stars and planets on human affairs. To comprehend its depth, one must first understand its basic components: signs, planets, houses, and aspects.

- **Signs**: The zodiac is divided into twelve signs, each representing a segment of the celestial sphere and associated with specific traits and tendencies. These signs are Aries, Taurus, Gemini, Cancer, Leo, Virgo, Libra, Scorpio, Sagittarius, Capricorn, Aquarius, and Pisces. Each sign is influenced by its ruling planet and element (fire, earth, air, or water), contributing to the sign's characteristic expressions in personality and life events.

- **Planets**: In astrology, planets are considered to wield significant influences, with each governing specific aspects of human life and character. From the personal planets like Mercury, Venus, and Mars to social planets Jupiter and Saturn, and beyond to generational bodies such as Uranus, Neptune, and Pluto, each plays a role in shaping our experiences and attributes.

- **Houses**: The astrological chart is divided into twelve houses, each representing a sphere of life, such as identity, resources, communication, home, pleasure, work, partnerships, transformation, philosophy, public status, community, and the subconscious. The placement of planets within these houses and their ruling signs further refines an individual's astrological profile.

- **Aspects**: Aspects are the angular relationships between planets in the horoscope, indicating how their energies combine and play out in one's life. Conjunctions, sextiles, squares, trines, and oppositions each tell a story of harmony, tension, ease, or challenge.

## Introduction to Plant Medicine and Hemp's Role Within It

Plant medicine refers to the use of plants' healing properties to prevent or cure illness and promote health and well-being. Across cultures and epochs, humans have turned to the flora around them for remedies, guided by both empirical knowledge and spiritual intuition. Hemp, with its versatile applications from medicinal to nutritional and industrial uses, occupies a significant place in plant medicine. Its cannabinoids, particularly CBD, have been recognized for therapeutic properties, including anti-inflammatory, anxiolytic, and neuroprotective effects.

## Astrological Aspects and the Effectiveness of Plant Medicine

The intricate dance of planets and signs can significantly influence the effectiveness of plant medicine, including hemp, in several ways:

- **Ruling Planets and Signs**: Plants, like hemp, are believed to be under the dominion of specific planets and signs, which influence their healing properties. For instance, a plant ruled by Venus might be particularly effective in treating conditions related to the kidneys, throat, or reproductive system, areas traditionally associated with Venusian energy.

- **Harvest and Preparation Timing**: The timing of harvesting and preparing plant medicines can be aligned with favorable astrological conditions to enhance their healing powers. For example, collecting hemp for CBD oil during a Moon in Taurus might imbue the preparation with stabilizing and grounding energies, given Taurus's earthy and Venus-ruled characteristics.

- **Personalized Medicine**: Just as our astrological charts highlight our unique susceptibilities and strengths, they can also guide the most beneficial plant medicines for our constitution. An individual with a prominent Mars may find relief in calming, Mars-opposed plant medicines, like hemp, to balance their fiery nature.

- **Planetary Transits and Healing Work**: The current positions of planets (transits) can activate parts of our natal chart, creating periods of particular sensitivity or strength. Utilizing plant medicine, including hemp, in harmony with these transits can support healing and growth. For instance, during a Neptune transit, which may heighten sensitivity, a person might benefit more from the soothing aspects of hemp.

**Conclusion: The Celestial and Terrestrial Synergy**

Astrology offers a rich framework for understanding our relationship with plant medicine, providing insights into how celestial influences can shape our interactions with the healing powers of nature. By exploring the astrological principles in the context of plant medicine, we unlock a more nuanced and personalized approach to health and wellness. Hemp, with its deep historical roots and broad medicinal applications, serves as a prime example of how we can integrate this ancient wisdom into our modern lives, harnessing the stars' power to enhance the healing nature of plants.

If you want to see some amazing products, please visit my Virtual Dispensary: https://shift.store/sg1fan23477/retail

**Chapter 3: Aries - The Pioneer's Plant**

In the constellation of the zodiac, Aries leads with the courage and vigor of a warrior, embodying the spirit of new beginnings and the fiery rush of enthusiasm. This chapter explores the dynamic synergy between Aries, the first sign of the zodiac, and hemp—a plant as versatile and pioneering as the individuals born under this sign. We delve into how specific strains of hemp can invigorate the energetic Aries, provide relief from their common ailments, and offer tips on integrating hemp into their wellness routine for optimal physical recovery.

**The Fiery Nature of Aries**

Aries, ruled by Mars, the planet of energy and action, are known for their boundless vitality, pioneering spirit, and, at times, their headstrong and impulsive nature. This cardinal fire sign thrives on challenge and often seeks out new and adventurous paths. However, their relentless drive can sometimes lead to burnout, headaches, and muscle pain, as they push their limits both mentally and physically.

**Hemp Strains That Stimulate Energy and Combat Fatigue**

For the energetic Aries seeking to maintain their natural zeal while managing the risk of overexertion, certain hemp strains can be particularly beneficial. Strains high in CBD are known for their ability to reduce inflammation and alleviate pain without the psychoactive effects associated with THC, making them an ideal choice for Aries looking to sustain their active lifestyle.

- **Sativa-dominant Hemp Strains**: These strains are renowned for their energizing effects, which can help combat fatigue—a common issue for Aries who rarely allow themselves time to rest. Strains such as Sour Space Candy or Lifter can provide a gentle boost of energy, enhancing focus and productivity, which aligns well with Aries' natural inclination towards action and achievement.

- **CBD-rich Strains**: For Aries, strains with a high CBD content like Elektra or ACDC can be particularly effective in managing inflammation and pain, common complaints among this active sign. These strains can help soothe muscle pain and stiffness, allowing Aries to bounce back more quickly from physical exertion.

### Hemp as a Tool for Aries' Headaches and Muscle Pain

Aries individuals often suffer from headaches and migraines, attributed to their ruled body part—the head. Incorporating hemp into their wellness regimen can offer a natural and effective remedy for these discomforts.

- **CBD Oils**: Taking CBD oil sublingually (under the tongue) can provide rapid relief for headaches, reducing inflammation and calming the intense energy that often contributes to Aries' head pain. Regular use may also help in reducing the frequency and intensity of headaches and migraines.
- **Hemp-infused Topicals**: For targeted muscle pain relief, hemp-infused topicals, such as creams and salves, can be applied directly to sore or tense areas. These products are particularly beneficial after intense physical activity, helping to alleviate discomfort and accelerate muscle recovery.

### Tips: Utilizing Hemp-Based Salves for Physical Recovery

Aries can incorporate hemp-based salves into their recovery routine with the following tips:

- **Post-Workout Application**: After a vigorous workout, apply a hemp-based salve to muscles that are prone to soreness. The anti-inflammatory properties of CBD can help to reduce swelling and pain, aiding in a quicker recovery.

- **Consistent Use**: For chronic issues, such as recurring headaches or muscle pains, consistent use of hemp-based products can offer cumulative benefits, gradually reducing the severity and frequency of these ailments.
- **Combine with Massage**: Enhance the effectiveness of hemp-based salves by combining their application with a gentle massage. This not only helps in the absorption of CBD but also promotes blood flow to the affected areas, further aiding in recovery and relaxation.

**Conclusion: Aries and the Energizing Power of Hemp**

For the bold and adventurous Aries, hemp offers a natural ally in sustaining their high energy levels, combating fatigue, and alleviating the physical pains that come with their active lifestyle. By selecting the right strains and incorporating hemp-based products into their wellness routines, Aries can continue to lead and innovate, fueled by the pioneering spirit of both themselves and the versatile hemp plant.

If you want to see some amazing products, please visit my Virtual Dispensary: https://shift.store/sg1fan23477/retail

## Chapter 4: Taurus - Grounding through Hemp

In the rich tapestry of the zodiac, Taurus stands out for its deep connection to the Earth, embodying qualities of stability, sensuality, and an appreciation for the finer things in life. Governed by Venus, the planet of love, beauty, and value, Taureans are drawn to comfort and pleasure, seeking both in the stability of their routines and the sensory experiences they cherish. This chapter delves into the symbiotic relationship between Taurus, a sign synonymous with groundedness, and hemp—a plant that mirrors Taurus's penchant for relaxation and sensory enrichment.

### The Essence of Taurus

Taureans are characterized by their steadfastness, reliability, and a love for all that is luxurious and comforting. This earth sign revels in the tactile and enjoys being surrounded by the best that life has to offer, from food to fabric. However, their love for comfort can sometimes lead to stress when their sense of stability is threatened, or when they find themselves unable to relax in the pursuit of their pleasures. Here, hemp steps in as a natural ally, offering Taurus a botanical means to achieve the relaxation and stress relief they seek, enhancing their sensory experiences and bolstering their innate need for stability.

### Preference for Strains that Promote Relaxation and Stress Relief

For Taurus, hemp strains that encourage relaxation and provide stress relief are particularly appealing, aligning with their desire for calm and serenity. Indica-dominant strains or those high in CBD can offer the tranquil experience Taureans crave:

- **Indica-dominant Hemp Strains**: Known for their relaxing effects, these strains can help soothe the body and mind, making them ideal for evening use when Taurus seeks to unwind and enjoy the tranquility of their sanctuaries.

- **High-CBD Strains:** Strains like Charlotte's Web and Harlequin, which boast a high CBD to THC ratio, are perfect for Taureans looking to alleviate anxiety without significant psychoactive effects. These strains can provide a gentle sense of calm and well-being, enhancing Taurus's natural propensity for relaxation.

## Hemp's Role in Enhancing Sensory Experiences and Stability for Taurus

Hemp can play a significant role in elevating the sensory experiences that are so valued by Taurus, adding a layer of depth and richness to their pursuit of pleasure:

- **Aromatic Hemp Infusions:** The aromatic properties of certain hemp strains can enhance the ambiance of a Taurus's living space, creating a comforting and sensually stimulating environment. Diffusing hemp essential oils or burning hemp-infused candles can envelop a Taurus in soothing scents, contributing to a serene and harmonious atmosphere.
- **Hemp Fabrics:** The tactile pleasure of hemp fabrics aligns with Taurus's love for luxurious textures. Incorporating hemp-based textiles into their wardrobe or home decor can satisfy their desire for comfort and sustainability, appealing to Taurus's sensibilities for quality and environmental consciousness.

## Tips: Incorporating Hemp Oils in Culinary Delights for a Grounded Sensation

For the culinary-minded Taurus, integrating hemp oils into their gastronomic creations can offer a novel way to enjoy the grounding properties of hemp while indulging their love for delightful flavors:

- **Salad Dressings and Sauces:** Hemp oil, with its nutty flavor, can be an exquisite addition to homemade salad dressings or sauces, enriching the taste profile of a dish while providing nutritional benefits, including essential fatty acids and antioxidants.

- **Baking with Hemp**: Incorporating hemp oil or hemp seeds into baked goods such as bread, cookies, or muffins can add a nutritious twist to Taurus's baking adventures, offering a satisfying and healthful indulgence.
- **Infused Beverages**: For a relaxing nightcap, Taureans can craft beverages infused with CBD oil, such as herbal teas or warm milk, to promote relaxation and a peaceful transition into sleep.

**Conclusion: Taurus and the Comforting Embrace of Hemp**

For Taurus, the grounding and sensory-enhancing qualities of hemp align perfectly with their zodiacal essence, offering a natural avenue to achieve the relaxation and stability they value so highly. By integrating hemp into their lives—be it through strains that promote relaxation, the aromatic and tactile pleasures of hemp-based products, or the incorporation of hemp oils into their culinary repertoire—Taureans can deepen their connection to the Earth and to themselves, finding comfort in the plant's versatile and grounding embrace.

If you want to see some amazing products, please visit my Virtual Dispensary: https://shift.store/sg1fan23477/retail

## Chapter 5: Gemini - The Communicator's Herb

In the zodiac's grand circle, Gemini, ruled by Mercury, stands as the quintessential communicator, embodying adaptability, intellectual curiosity, and a vibrant social nature. This air sign thrives on exchange —be it ideas, stories, or laughter—and possesses an innate restlessness that propels them through life's myriad experiences. This chapter explores the relationship between Gemini and hemp, focusing on how certain strains can complement Gemini's multifaceted personality by enhancing mood and social engagement while providing relief from their common nervous system challenges.

### Gemini's Versatile Nature

Gemini's are known for their dual nature, often juggling multiple interests, hobbies, and social circles simultaneously. Their quick wit and intellectual prowess make them excellent conversationalists, while their versatility allows them to adapt seamlessly to varying situations. However, this constant mental and social activity can sometimes lead to anxiety, restlessness, and a scattered focus, underscoring the need for balance through natural aids like hemp.

### Matching Strains for Mood Enhancement and Social Engagement

For Geminis, engaging with the right hemp strains can significantly enhance their social experiences and mood, aligning with their need for mental stimulation and variety:

- **Sativa-dominant Strains**: Known for their uplifting and energizing effects, sativa-dominant strains are ideal for Geminis. Strains such as Super Lemon Haze or Jack Herer can invigorate the mind, spark creativity, and foster the lively conversation that Geminis crave, making social gatherings more enjoyable and stimulating.
- **CBD-rich Strains**: For those Geminis looking to mitigate the edge of their natural nervous energy without dampening their sociability, CBD-rich strains like Sour Tsunami or Cannatonic

can offer a calming effect. These strains help in smoothing out the anxiety that can accompany Gemini's rapid-fire thought process, facilitating a more relaxed yet engaging social interaction.

**Using Hemp to Aid with Gemini's Nervous System Challenges**

Given Gemini's propensity for anxiety and restlessness—side effects of their active minds and constant quest for stimulation—hemp can serve as a valuable tool in managing these challenges:

- **CBD Oils**: Regular use of CBD oil can provide Geminis with a steadying influence, reducing anxiety levels and aiding in focus. Its non-psychoactive properties mean it can be used throughout the day, helping to maintain a balanced state of mind without interfering with their dynamic lifestyle.
- **Microdosing THC**: For Geminis who are THC tolerant, microdosing strains with a balanced THC/CBD ratio can offer the benefits of mood elevation and creativity enhancement without overwhelming their system, keeping them grounded yet inspired.

**Tips: Vaping Sativa-dominant Strains for a Quick Mood Lift**

Vaping sativa-dominant strains can be an effective method for Geminis seeking a quick mood lift or a spark of creativity, especially before social events or brainstorming sessions:

- **Portable Vaping**: Geminis' on-the-go lifestyle makes portable vaporizers an excellent choice for enjoying their preferred strains discreetly and conveniently, allowing for quick mood adjustments wherever they are.
- **Temperature Settings**: Experimenting with different temperature settings can help Geminis fine-tune their vaping experience, with lower temperatures preserving the strain's flavor and terpenes for a more cerebral effect, ideal for stimulating conversation and creativity.

- **Strain Rotation:** To keep in step with Gemini's love for variety, rotating between different sativa-dominant strains can prevent tolerance buildup and keep the experience fresh and engaging, mirroring their ever-changing interests and moods.

## Conclusion: Gemini and the Elevating Power of Hemp

For the socially adept and intellectually curious Gemini, hemp presents a natural complement to their dynamic essence. By carefully selecting strains that enhance mood and social engagement while addressing the nervous system's challenges, Geminis can navigate their multifaceted lives with greater ease and joy. Through the judicious use of sativa-dominant strains and CBD-rich options, alongside innovative consumption methods like vaping, Geminis can harness the communicative and mood-lifting powers of hemp, making it truly the communicator's herb.

If you want to see some amazing products, please visit my Virtual Dispensary: https://shift.store/sg1fan23477/retail

**Chapter 6: Cancer - Emotional Healing with Hemp**

Within the zodiac, Cancer represents the archetype of the nurturer, characterized by deep emotional sensitivity, empathy, and an intrinsic need for comfort and security. Ruled by the Moon, this water sign experiences the ebbs and flows of emotions more intensely than any other, making their journey through life rich with feelings. This chapter navigates the soothing potential of hemp for Cancerians, focusing on strains that offer calm and comfort, the plant's role in easing digestive issues tied to emotional stress, and crafting a self-care routine that harnesses hemp's emotional healing properties.

**Cancer's Emotional Depth**

Cancerians possess an unparalleled emotional depth, with a strong inclination toward nurturing and caring for others. Their empathetic nature, however, can sometimes lead to emotional overwhelm, making them susceptible to stress, anxiety, and mood fluctuations. Furthermore, as Cancer rules the stomach, emotional turmoil can often manifest as digestive issues, highlighting the need for holistic healing approaches that address both their emotional and physical well-being.

**Hemp Strains for Calming and Comforting**

Selecting the right hemp strains can significantly aid Cancerians in finding their emotional equilibrium, providing a sense of calm and comfort amidst the storm of their feelings:

- **Indica-dominant Strains**: Known for their relaxing effects, indica-dominant strains can be particularly beneficial for Cancerians seeking to unwind and find peace in their often turbulent emotional waters. Strains like Granddaddy Purple or Northern Lights can offer a tranquil escape, easing anxiety and fostering a sense of serenity.

- **High-CBD Strains**: CBD-rich strains such as Charlotte's Web and Harlequin are excellent for managing stress and anxiety without inducing psychoactive effects. These strains can help Cancerians maintain a balanced mood, alleviating emotional distress while allowing them to remain fully present and engaged in their daily lives.

## Hemp's Role in Aiding Digestive Issues

The stress and anxiety that Cancerians frequently encounter can lead to digestive discomfort and issues, given their emotional connection to their stomach. Hemp can offer a natural remedy:

- **CBD Oils**: Incorporating CBD oil into their wellness regimen can help Cancerians manage stress-induced digestive problems. CBD's anti-inflammatory properties can soothe the digestive tract, alleviating symptoms like cramping, bloating, and inflammation.
- **Hemp Seeds**: Rich in fiber, hemp seeds can be a beneficial addition to the diet of a Cancerian dealing with digestive issues. They can help promote digestive health, offering a gentle, natural way to ease discomfort and support overall gut wellness.

## Tips: Creating a Hemp-Infused Self-Care Routine for Emotional Wellness

For Cancerians, developing a self-care routine that incorporates hemp can be a deeply nurturing practice, offering a path to emotional and physical healing:

- **Hemp Tea for Relaxation**: Brewing a comforting cup of hemp tea can be a soothing ritual for Cancerians, especially in the evening. The warmth and herbal benefits of the tea can help calm the mind and prepare the body for rest, enhancing emotional well-being.

- **CBD Bath Bombs**: Integrating CBD-infused bath bombs into a self-care routine can provide a luxurious and therapeutic experience. The combination of warm water, CBD, and essential oils can deeply relax the body, ease muscle tension, and promote a state of emotional tranquility.
- **Journaling with CBD**: Engaging in reflective journaling while enjoying the benefits of CBD, either through oils, vapes, or edibles, can facilitate emotional processing and release. This practice can help Cancerians navigate their feelings more effectively, fostering a sense of clarity and emotional balance.

**Conclusion: Cancer and the Path to Emotional Healing with Hemp**

For the emotionally attuned Cancer, hemp offers a gentle yet powerful ally in navigating the depths of their feelings and the physical manifestations of stress. By choosing strains that provide calm and comfort, addressing digestive wellness, and incorporating hemp into a holistic self-care routine, Cancerians can find a more peaceful and balanced way to engage with their emotional world. Through the nurturing embrace of hemp, Cancer offers a model of emotional healing and self-care that resonates with the heart of their watery essence.

If you want to see some amazing products, please visit my Virtual Dispensary: https://shift.store/sg1fan23477/retail

## Chapter 7: Leo - Radiance and Recovery

In the celestial realm, Leo shines with a brilliance that mirrors their ruling luminary, the Sun. Characterized by their boldness, creativity, and an unyielding zest for life, Leos are the natural performers of the zodiac, basking in the spotlight and energizing those around them with their fiery spirit. This chapter delves into the synergistic relationship between Leo and hemp, highlighting strains that bolster heart health and vitality, the anti-inflammatory benefits that support Leo's dynamic physicality, and practical tips for integrating hemp seed snacks into their diet for enhanced energy and cardiovascular wellness.

### Leo's Vivacity and Heart Health

Leos are renowned for their vivacious energy and strong desire to express themselves creatively and passionately. Governed by the heart both metaphorically and anatomically, they often pour their entire being into their pursuits. However, this intense exertion—both emotional and physical—can sometimes strain their cardiovascular health. Herein lies the potential for hemp to play a vital role in supporting the heart and overall vitality of Leos, ensuring that they continue to radiate their inherent light without compromise.

### Selection of Strains for Vitality and Heart Health

To match Leo's vibrant energy and support their heart health, specific hemp strains and products can be particularly beneficial:

- **CBD-rich Strains**: CBD has been recognized for its potential to lower high blood pressure, a common risk factor for heart disease. Strains like Ringo's Gift or ACDC can provide Leos with the CBD content they need to help manage stress levels and support cardiovascular health, allowing them to shine brightly without undue strain on their hearts.
- **Balanced THC/CBD Strains**: For Leos who appreciate the euphoric uplift that THC offers but still seek the balancing effects of CBD, strains such as Harle-Tsu or Cannatonic can offer a

harmonious blend. These strains can enhance Leo's natural vitality and creativity while contributing to their overall well-being.

### Hemp's Anti-inflammatory Properties to Support Leo's Physical Presence

Leo's dynamic lifestyle and penchant for being in the limelight mean that maintaining a strong and healthy physical presence is paramount. The anti-inflammatory properties of hemp can be particularly advantageous in supporting this aspect of Leo's life:

- **Topical Hemp Products**: For localized relief from muscle soreness or joint pain resulting from Leo's active endeavors, topical hemp products like creams and salves can provide targeted anti-inflammatory benefits, helping to ensure that nothing dims their radiant energy.
- **Full-Spectrum Hemp Oil**: Incorporating full-spectrum hemp oil into their wellness regimen can offer systemic anti-inflammatory benefits, potentially aiding in recovery after physical exertion and reducing the risk of chronic inflammation-related issues.

### Tips: Hemp Seed Snacks for Energy and Cardiovascular Health

For Leos, whose lifestyle demands a constant reservoir of energy, incorporating hemp seed snacks into their diet can offer a nutritious boost:

- **Hemp Seed Energy Bars**: Homemade or store-bought energy bars containing hemp seeds can provide a quick and convenient source of protein, essential fatty acids, and fiber, all of which are crucial for sustained energy levels and heart health.
- **Hemp Seed Smoothies**: Adding a tablespoon of hemp seeds or hemp protein powder to morning smoothies can kickstart Leo's day with a nutrient-rich beverage, supporting cardiovascular health and providing the necessary fuel for their adventures.

- **Hemp Heart Toppings**: Sprinkling hemp hearts over salads, yogurt, or oatmeal can effortlessly increase Leo's intake of omega-3 and omega-6 fatty acids, supporting heart health and overall vitality.

**Conclusion: Leo's Journey with Hemp - Radiance and Recovery**

For the radiant Leo, integrating hemp into their lifestyle can play a significant role in supporting their heart health, enhancing vitality, and aiding in recovery from their boundless endeavors. By selecting the right strains and incorporating hemp-based products and snacks into their diet, Leos can safeguard their physical well-being while continuing to shine and inspire those around them with their indomitable spirit. In the embrace of hemp, Leo finds a supportive ally, ensuring that their light remains as brilliant and invigorating as ever.

If you want to see some amazing products, please visit my Virtual Dispensary: https://shift.store/sg1fan23477/retail

## Chapter 8: Virgo - The Purist's Prescription

In the zodiac's intricate mosaic, Virgo emerges as the emblem of meticulousness, purity, and an unwavering dedication to health and wellness. Ruled by Mercury, this earth sign harnesses a profound analytical ability, applying it with precision to all aspects of life, particularly those concerning health and wellbeing. This chapter explores Virgo's harmonious relationship with hemp, focusing on CBD-rich strains that align with their predilection for purity, the role of hemp in supporting gut health—a frequent area of focus for health-conscious Virgos—and practical tips for incorporating hemp-based CBD supplements into their daily wellness regimen.

### Virgo's Analytical Approach to Health

Virgos possess an innate propensity for analysis and detail, which extends into their approach to health and wellness. They often exhibit an interest in holistic health, preferring natural and pure remedies to maintain their wellbeing. This preference makes hemp, especially CBD-rich strains known for their therapeutic benefits without psychoactive effects, particularly appealing to Virgo's purist inclinations.

### Preference for CBD-rich Strains for Precision and Purity

For Virgos, the allure of CBD-rich hemp strains lies in their ability to deliver clear, therapeutic benefits without the cloudiness of THC-induced psychoactivity. This aligns perfectly with Virgo's desire for control and precision in health matters:

- **High-CBD Strains**: Varieties such as Charlotte's Web and Harlequin provide the high CBD content that Virgos value for its potential to alleviate anxiety, inflammation, and pain, facilitating a focused and productive state of mind that Virgos appreciate.

- **CBD Isolates**: For those Virgos who are especially sensitive to THC or who prefer the most refined form of supplementation, CBD isolate products can offer a pure, targeted approach to symptom relief and overall wellness, aligning with their penchant for specificity.

**Utilizing Hemp for Gut Health and Meticulous Dietary Planning**

Virgo's rulership over the digestive system points to a common focus on gut health within this sign. The anti-inflammatory and homeostatic properties of hemp can be particularly beneficial in this regard:

- **Hemp Seeds and Oil**: Rich in omega-3 and omega-6 fatty acids, hemp seeds and hemp seed oil can support digestive health by reducing inflammation in the gut and aiding in the maintenance of the intestinal lining. Incorporating these into meals aligns with Virgo's meticulous dietary planning, offering a simple yet effective way to bolster gut health.
- **CBD for Digestive Balance**: CBD's interaction with the endocannabinoid system, which plays a key role in maintaining gut homeostasis, can help manage digestive issues such as inflammation and discomfort, a boon for the health-focused Virgo.

**Tips: Incorporating Hemp-Based CBD Supplements for Daily Wellness**

Virgos can enhance their wellness routine and maintain their high standards of health and purity by incorporating hemp-based CBD supplements with the following tips:

- **Daily CBD Tinctures**: For a precise and easy-to-adjust dosage, CBD tinctures can be integrated into the Virgo's morning routine, offering a foundation of calm and focus for the day ahead.

- **Hemp Seed Additions**: Virgos can add hemp seeds to their meals, such as sprinkling on salads, blending into smoothies, or incorporating into yogurt, for a nutritious boost that supports their detailed dietary requirements.
- **Topical CBD for Targeted Relief**: For localized issues such as muscle soreness or skin conditions, CBD-infused topical products can offer direct, measurable relief, fitting seamlessly into Virgo's regimen of personal care and health maintenance.

**Conclusion: Virgo and the Path to Purity with Hemp**

For the meticulous Virgo, hemp, particularly in its CBD-rich forms, presents a natural extension of their holistic approach to health and wellness. By embracing the precision and purity offered by CBD, whether through strains, isolates, or dietary supplements, Virgos can find a natural ally in their quest for optimal health. Through careful incorporation into their daily routine, hemp stands as a testament to Virgo's dedication to wellbeing, reflecting their analytical yet nurturing spirit in the pursuit of a balanced and healthy life.

If you want to see some amazing products, please visit my Virtual Dispensary: https://shift.store/sg1fan23477/retail

## Chapter 9: Libra - Balance in Bloom

In the zodiac's grand theatre, Libra occupies the stage of harmony, beauty, and partnership, under the graceful governance of Venus. This air sign embodies the quest for balance, seeking equilibrium in all aspects of life, from social interactions to personal health and aesthetics. Libra's intrinsic connection to Venus endows them with a keen eye for beauty, making them admirers of harmony not just in relationships but in their environment and self-presentation as well. This chapter delves into the unique resonance between Libra and hemp, highlighting strains that foster social and skin health, the significance of hemp in supporting kidney function and harmonious partnerships, and practical advice on incorporating hemp-infused skincare to enhance Libra's natural allure.

### Libra's Quest for Equilibrium

For Libra, life is an endless pursuit of balance. This sign thrives in peaceful, harmonious environments and strives to maintain equilibrium in their relationships and within themselves. However, this constant balancing act can sometimes lead to stress and anxiety, especially when harmony is disrupted. In such instances, Libra seeks solace in natural remedies that can restore their inner peace without tipping the scales.

### Strains that Enhance Social Harmony and Skin Health

Libra's social nature and Venusian influence make them gravitate towards strains that not only enhance social interactions but also support their skin's health, reflecting their inner balance outwardly:

- **CBD-rich Strains**: Strains with a high CBD content, such as ACDC or Cannatonic, are ideal for Libras. CBD's calming properties can ease social anxiety, making Libras feel more comfortable and balanced in social settings. Additionally, CBD's anti-inflammatory and antioxidative properties can contribute to skin health, aligning with Libra's aesthetic values.

- **Balanced THC/CBD Strains**: Strains that offer a balanced ratio of THC and CBD can provide the mild euphoria and relaxation that enhances Libra's social experiences, without overwhelming them. Harlequin, for instance, can stimulate conversation and laughter, making social gatherings more enjoyable and balanced.

## The Role of Hemp in Maintaining Kidney Balance and Partnerships

Libra rules the kidneys, organs integral to maintaining the body's balance by filtering waste and excess fluids. The stress of constantly seeking equilibrium, however, can impact this critical balancing act within the body. Hemp's role in supporting kidney function and thereby contributing to overall homeostasis is of particular interest to Libras:

- **Hemp Oil for Kidney Health**: The omega-3 fatty acids in hemp seed oil can support kidney health by reducing inflammation and potentially lowering blood pressure, both of which are beneficial for the kidneys. Incorporating hemp oil into the diet can thus play a part in Libra's broader health strategy focused on balance and wellness.
- **CBD for Stress Relief**: By mitigating stress and promoting a sense of calm, CBD can indirectly support kidney health, as stress can exacerbate conditions that burden the kidneys. For Libras, managing stress is thus doubly important, and CBD can be a valuable tool in their wellness arsenal.

## Tips: Using Hemp-Infused Skincare to Enhance Libra's Natural Allure

Libra's affinity for beauty and self-care makes hemp-infused skincare products a perfect addition to their routine, helping to maintain skin health and complement their natural allure:

- **Hemp-Infused Moisturizers**: Daily use of hemp-infused moisturizers can hydrate and nourish the skin, thanks to hemp oil's balance of essential fatty acids. These moisturizers can help improve skin's elasticity and reduce redness, keeping Libra's skin glowing and balanced.
- **CBD Facial Serums**: For targeted skin concerns, CBD facial serums can offer potent anti-inflammatory and antioxidative benefits, addressing issues like acne, sensitivity, and premature aging. The serums can fit seamlessly into Libra's skincare regimen, providing a luxurious and effective treatment that mirrors their quest for beauty and balance.
- **Hemp Body Oils**: A soothing hemp body oil can envelop Libra in a sense of overall well-being, nourishing the skin and promoting a harmonious balance between mind and body. The sensual experience of applying hemp body oil can also be a moment of self-care that aligns with Libra's Venusian essence.

## Conclusion: Libra and the Harmony of Hemp

For Libra, hemp presents a multifaceted ally in their pursuit of balance, offering benefits that extend from enhancing social grace to supporting physical health and beauty. By choosing strains and products that align with their quest for equilibrium and Venusian qualities, Libras can integrate hemp into their lives as a means of achieving the harmony they so deeply desire. In the world of hemp, Libra finds a partner in balance, echoing the sign's innate affinity for peace, partnership, and natural allure.

If you want to see some amazing products, please visit my Virtual Dispensary: https://shift.store/sg1fan23477/retail

## Chapter 10: Scorpio - Transformational Tinctures

Scorpio, a sign enveloped in mystery and depth, navigates the waters of existence with unparalleled intensity and emotional profundity. Ruled by Pluto, the planet of transformation and regeneration, Scorpios are drawn to experiences that challenge the depths of their being, seeking transformation and rebirth through their encounters with the shadowy aspects of life. This chapter explores the profound connection between Scorpio and hemp, focusing on potent strains that facilitate deep healing and emotional exploration, the plant's contributions to sexual health and rejuvenation, and practical tips on leveraging hemp oil for hormonal balance and enhanced intimacy.

### Scorpio's Intensity and the Choice of Potent Strains

The intense nature of Scorpios demands strains that are equally profound, capable of catalyzing the deep healing and introspection that this sign so often seeks:

- **Potent THC Strains**: For Scorpios who can handle the psychoactive effects, high-THC strains may offer the psychological depth and intensity they crave, facilitating a journey into the subconscious and aiding in the exploration of their inner worlds. Strains like Gorilla Glue or Blue Dream can offer the potent experience sought by Scorpios, aiding in emotional release and exploration.

- **CBD-dominant Strains for Healing**: Understanding that transformation often requires healing, CBD-dominant strains like Charlotte's Web and ACDC can provide Scorpios with a grounding influence, offering relief from the emotional and physical pain that may accompany their journey of self-discovery and transformation without overwhelming psychoactivity.

**Hemp's Role in Sexual Health and Regeneration**

Scorpio, a sign also associated with sexuality and the reproductive system, finds a natural ally in hemp for supporting sexual health and fostering regeneration:

- **Enhancing Intimacy**: Hemp oil, particularly when infused with CBD, can enhance intimacy and sexual health by alleviating anxiety and improving blood flow. These benefits can lead to more relaxed and satisfying sexual experiences, aligning with Scorpio's desire for deep, transformative connections.
- **Supporting Reproductive Health**: The anti-inflammatory properties of CBD may also offer benefits for reproductive health, potentially easing discomfort associated with conditions like endometriosis or menstrual cramps, which aligns with Scorpio's regenerative powers.

**Tips: Exploring Hemp Oil's Benefits for Hormonal Balance and Intimacy**

Scorpios looking to harness the transformational properties of hemp for hormonal balance and enhanced intimacy can consider the following tips:

- **Daily CBD Supplementation**: Integrating CBD oil into daily routines can help maintain hormonal balance, reduce stress, and alleviate anxiety, laying a foundation for healthy sexual function and deeper intimacy.
- **Topical Hemp Oil for Intimacy**: Hemp oil can be used as a natural lubricant, enhancing physical comfort and emotional connection during intimate moments. Its moisturizing properties can also support skin health, adding a sensual dimension to its use.
- **Hemp-infused Massage Oils**: Incorporating hemp-infused massage oils into foreplay or relaxation routines can deepen the emotional and physical connection between partners, promoting

intimacy through the power of touch while benefiting from the soothing and regenerative properties of hemp.

**Conclusion: Scorpio and the Power of Transformational Tinctures**

For Scorpio, the path of transformation is both a challenge and a calling, requiring tools that can match their intensity and depth. Hemp, with its potent strains for deep emotional exploration, its supportive role in sexual health and regeneration, and its capacity to facilitate hormonal balance and intimacy, emerges as a powerful ally in Scorpio's transformative journey. By engaging with the profound and versatile benefits of hemp, Scorpios can navigate their deep waters with greater ease, embracing the regenerative potential that defines their very essence. In the realm of hemp, Scorpios find not just a remedy but a partner in their ceaseless quest for rebirth and renewal.

For everything for any Zodiac sign can get Hemp infused Lubes, and Hemp infused Sexual Enhancement at my Virtual Dispensary, why let The Stigma of Hemp and The Stigma of Sexual please be Taboo? If you want to see some amazing products, please visit my Virtual Dispensary: https://shift.store/sg1fan23477/retail

**Chapter 11: Sagittarius - The Explorer's Elixir**

Sagittarius, the archer of the zodiac, embarks on life's journey with an insatiable thirst for adventure, wisdom, and freedom. Governed by Jupiter, the planet of expansion and exploration, those born under this sign are natural philosophers, travelers, and seekers of truth. Their journey is not just about physical travel but also the exploration of ideas and the expansion of their own consciousness. This chapter explores the relationship between Sagittarius and hemp, focusing on strains that fuel inspiration and broaden horizons, the plant's role in supporting liver health—an organ significantly ruled by Sagittarius—and practical tips for incorporating hemp into travel routines to alleviate jet lag and bolster immunity.

**Sagittarius's Adventurous Spirit and Strains for Inspiration and Expansion**

For the Sagittarian explorer, certain hemp strains can act as catalysts for inspiration and aid in the quest for knowledge and personal growth:

- **Sativa-dominant Strains**: With their uplifting and energizing effects, sativa strains are perfectly aligned with the Sagittarian spirit. Strains like Sour Diesel and Super Silver Haze can stimulate creativity, enhance mental clarity, and encourage philosophical musing, complementing Sagittarius's expansive nature.
- **Strains with Pinene Terpenes**: Strains high in the terpene pinene, known for its ability to improve alertness and memory retention, can be particularly beneficial for Sagittarians engaged in intellectual pursuits or when exploring new cultures and philosophies.

**Hemp Supports Liver Health and Philosophical Pursuits**

The liver, a crucial organ for detoxification and metabolism, falls under Sagittarius's domain. The sign's propensity for indulgence can sometimes lead to excess, making liver health a priority:

- **CBD for Liver Support:** Research suggests that CBD may have protective effects on the liver, helping to mitigate inflammation and oxidative stress. For Sagittarians, incorporating CBD oil or tinctures into their wellness regimen can support liver health, ensuring that their adventurous spirit is not weighed down by physical constraints.

- **Hemp Seeds for Nutritional Support:** Rich in essential fatty acids and antioxidants, hemp seeds can be a valuable dietary addition for maintaining liver health and overall vitality. Their high nutritional value supports Sagittarius's dynamic lifestyle and quest for adventure.

**Tips: Integrating Hemp into Travel Routines for Jet Lag and Immunity**

Sagittarians are the travelers of the zodiac, often crossing time zones and exploring distant lands. Hemp can be an invaluable companion on these journeys, offering relief from jet lag and enhancing immunity:

- **CBD Capsules for Jet Lag:** CBD can help regulate sleep cycles disrupted by travel, easing the transition across time zones. Sagittarians can take CBD capsules a few hours before bedtime to promote restful sleep and combat jet lag.

- **Hemp-derived CBD Gummies for Immune Support:** CBD has been recognized for its anti-inflammatory properties and potential to support the immune system. Consuming hemp-derived CBD gummies during travel can provide a convenient and discreet way to bolster Sagittarius's immunity, protecting them as they embrace the unknown.

- **Topical CBD for Muscle Fatigue**: Long hours of travel can lead to muscle stiffness and discomfort. CBD-infused topicals can be applied to tired legs and sore shoulders to alleviate pain, making the exploration of new terrains more comfortable and enjoyable.

**Conclusion: Sagittarius and the Explorer's Elixir**

For Sagittarius, the journey through life is a boundless quest for knowledge, freedom, and growth. Hemp, with its strains that spark inspiration, its capacity to support liver health, and its versatility in travel wellness routines, emerges as the explorer's elixir. By aligning with hemp's multifaceted benefits, Sagittarians can embrace their adventures with enhanced vitality, clarity, and resilience, ensuring that their spirited quest for expansion is as enriching as it is boundless. In the vast expanse of the universe, Sagittarius finds in hemp a companion for the journey, a botanical ally that supports both the physical and philosophical voyages that define the essence of the archer.

If you want to see some amazing products, please visit my Virtual Dispensary: https://shift.store/sg1fan23477/retail

**Chapter 12: Capricorn - The Achiever's Ally**

Capricorn, the zodiac's tenacious mountain goat, climbs life's steep paths with unmatched ambition and discipline. Ruled by Saturn, the planet of structure, responsibility, and hard work, Capricorns are the architects of their own destinies, building their successes with patience and perseverance. This chapter uncovers the symbiotic relationship between Capricorn and hemp, focusing on strains that enhance focus and support bone health, the role of hemp in managing the stress of their ceaseless endeavors, and tips for integrating hemp protein into fitness regimens to fortify muscle and bone strength, aligning with Capricorn's steadfast pursuit of their goals.

**Capricorn's Ambition and the Use of Hemp Strains for Focus, Bone Health, and Discipline**

Capricorn's earth-bound journey is marked by a relentless drive for achievement, necessitating aids that can enhance their natural focus and support their physical well-being:

- **CBD-dominant Strains for Focus**: For the Capricorn seeking to maintain their sharp focus and clarity, CBD-dominant strains such as Charlotte's Web and Harlequin can offer the concentration needed to tackle their ambitious projects without the distracting high associated with THC.
- **Strains with Myrcene for Bone Health**: Research suggests that certain terpenes, like myrcene, found in hemp may have benefits for bone health and healing. Strains rich in myrcene, such as Special Sauce and Mango Kush, can be beneficial for Capricorns, supporting their skeletal system as they navigate their demanding pursuits.

**The Importance of Hemp in Capricorn's Routine for Stress Management**

The weight of Capricorn's aspirations can often lead to high levels of stress, making stress management not just a necessity but a priority for maintaining their health and productivity:

- **Hemp Oil for Stress Relief**: The anxiolytic properties of CBD found in hemp oil can be a significant aid in Capricorn's stress management routine, offering a natural way to relax and unwind after a day of hard work, thus preserving their mental and emotional well-being.
- **Full-Spectrum Hemp Products for Overall Wellness**: Full-spectrum hemp products, containing CBD along with other cannabinoids and terpenes, can provide a holistic effect, potentially enhancing mood and reducing stress, aiding Capricorn in maintaining their balance.

**Tips: Employing Hemp Protein in Fitness Regimens for Muscle and Bone Strength**

Understanding Capricorn's appreciation for discipline and their focus on long-term health and fitness goals, integrating hemp protein into their dietary regimen can offer numerous benefits:

- **Hemp Protein for Muscle Recovery**: High in protein and essential amino acids, hemp protein is an excellent supplement for post-workout recovery, aiding in muscle repair and growth, which is crucial for Capricorns who engage in regular physical activity as part of their disciplined lifestyle.
- **Incorporating Hemp Seeds for Calcium and Magnesium**: Hemp seeds are a rich source of minerals like calcium and magnesium, essential for bone health and strength. Capricorns can add hemp seeds to their diets, through smoothies, salads, or as

a topping, to ensure their skeletal system receives the support it needs to sustain their active and ambitious lifestyle.

- **Hemp Oil for Inflammation**: Including hemp oil in their diet can help Capricorns manage inflammation, supporting joint health and mobility, which is vital for their continuous climb towards their goals.

## Conclusion: Capricorn and The Achiever's Ally

For Capricorn, the journey towards achievement is a marathon, not a sprint, requiring not just relentless drive but also tools that support their mental focus, physical health, and stress management. Hemp emerges as the achiever's ally, offering strains and products that align with Capricorn's disciplined approach to life and work. By integrating hemp into their wellness and fitness routines, Capricorns can maintain the strength, focus, and equilibrium necessary to conquer their lofty ambitions, ensuring that their journey is as sustainable as it is successful. In hemp, Capricorn finds a companion for the climb, a botanical ally that supports their foundation as they reach for the summit of their aspirations.

If you want to see some amazing products, please visit my Virtual Dispensary: https://shift.store/sg1fan23477/retail

**Chapter 13: Aquarius - The Innovator's Infusion**

Aquarius, the zodiac's bearer of water and wisdom, flows through life with an innovative spirit and a vision for the future that often places them ahead of their time. Ruled by Uranus, the planet of breakthroughs and revolutionary ideas, Aquarians are the trailblazers and visionaries of the zodiac, dedicated to progress, community, and the betterment of society. This chapter delves into the unique alignment between Aquarius and hemp, highlighting strains that spark creativity and support neurological health, the plant's contributions to circulatory health and communal wellness initiatives, and creative tips for integrating hemp-infused beverages into social and intellectual gatherings.

**Aquarius's Visionary Qualities and Hemp Strains for Creativity and Neurological Health**

Aquarius thrives on innovation and creative problem-solving, seeking strains that can unlock the doors to new ideas and enhance mental agility:

- **Sativa-dominant Strains for Creativity**: Strains like Green Crack and Super Lemon Haze, known for their uplifting and energizing effects, can stimulate Aquarius's already active mind, fostering creativity and aiding in the flow of revolutionary ideas.
- **CBD for Neurological Health**: Given Aquarius's ruler Uranus's association with the nervous system, CBD's neuroprotective properties can be particularly beneficial. Strains high in CBD, such as ACDC or Harle-Tsu, can support neurological health, ensuring Aquarius's innovative mind remains sharp and resilient.

**Leveraging Hemp for Circulatory Health and Community Wellness Projects**

Aquarius, with their humanitarian leanings, not only seeks personal health and wellness but also aims to uplift their communities. Hemp can play a role in both:

- **Hemp Seeds for Heart Health**: Rich in omega-3 and omega-6 fatty acids, hemp seeds can support circulatory health, a boon for the water-bearer concerned with maintaining a healthy flow of ideas and innovation. Including hemp seeds in the diet can help improve heart health, aligning with Aquarius's focus on longevity and vitality.

- **Community Wellness Initiatives**: Aquarians can lead community projects that incorporate hemp into public health initiatives, such as creating community gardens to grow hemp or organizing workshops on the benefits of hemp for sustainable living, harnessing their visionary qualities for the collective good.

**Tips: Crafting Hemp-Infused Beverages for Social Gatherings and Brainstorming Sessions**

Aquarius's social circles often revolve around intellectual exchange and envisioning future possibilities. Here are some creative ways to integrate hemp into these gatherings:

- **Hemp Seed Milk Smoothies**: Blend hemp seed milk with fruits, greens, and superfoods for a nutritious smoothie to fuel the body and mind during brainstorming sessions or workshops, providing the essential fatty acids and proteins needed for sustained mental energy.

- **CBD-infused Teas**: Crafting CBD-infused herbal teas can add a calming yet mentally engaging element to social gatherings, facilitating deeper conversation and creative exchange. Ingredients like peppermint or ginkgo biloba can complement CBD's effects, enhancing mental clarity and focus.

- **Hemp-infused Cold Brews**: For a refreshing twist, Aquarians can prepare hemp-infused cold brew coffee for meetings or social activism events, offering an energizing beverage that stimulates discussion and keeps the innovative ideas flowing.

**Conclusion: Aquarius and The Innovator's Infusion**

For the forward-thinking Aquarius, hemp serves as both a muse and a medium for health, innovation, and community engagement. By selecting strains that fuel creativity and support neurological and circulatory health, and by creatively incorporating hemp into social and communal settings, Aquarians can harness the plant's versatile benefits to propel their visionary pursuits. Hemp-infused beverages, in particular, offer a novel way to blend Aquarius's love for community with their penchant for innovation, making every sip a testament to the possibilities that lie at the intersection of wellness and progress. In the visionary waters of Aquarius, hemp finds its ideal role as an innovator's infusion, a catalyst for change that flows as freely and as boundlessly as the ideas of the water-bearer itself.

If you want to see some amazing products, please visit my Virtual Dispensary: https://shift.store/sg1fan23477/retail

**Chapter 14: Pisces - The Mystic's Medicine**

Pisces, the zodiac's final sign, swims in the deep waters of the unconscious, embodying intuition, sensitivity, and a profound spiritual connection. Ruled by Neptune, the planet of dreams, mysticism, and illusions, Pisceans navigate the world with an otherworldly perspective, often seeking solace and meaning in the metaphysical realm. This chapter explores the intimate relationship between Pisces and hemp, spotlighting strains that foster spiritual connections and relaxation, the plant's efficacy in addressing foot-related concerns intrinsic to Pisces, and practical advice on incorporating hemp teas into bedtime rituals to encourage restful sleep and vivid dreams.

**Pisces's Sensitivity and the Selection of Strains for Spiritual Connection and Relaxation**

Pisces's ethereal nature draws them towards strains that not only soothe their emotional waters but also enhance their spiritual receptivity:

- **Indica-dominant Strains for Relaxation**: To calm their often turbulent emotional and psychic seas, Pisces may find solace in indica-dominant strains, such as Granddaddy Purple or Northern Lights, which can provide the deep relaxation necessary for spiritual introspection and connection.
- **High-CBD Strains for Spiritual Clarity**: CBD-rich strains like Ringo's Gift or Charlotte's Web can offer Pisces the clarity and tranquility needed to navigate their rich inner lives without the overwhelming psychoactive effects that might cloud their introspection.

**Using Hemp to Combat Foot Issues and for Dream Enhancement**

As the sign associated with the feet, Pisces may experience sensitivity or issues in this area, reflecting the burdens of their empathetic nature. Additionally, their ruling planet Neptune's domain over dreams makes dream enhancement a coveted benefit:

- **Topical Hemp Products for Foot Care**: CBD-infused creams and balms can be applied to the feet to relieve pain, inflammation, or discomfort, aiding Pisces in their physical journey as much as their spiritual one. This topical application can provide the care their sensitive feet need after carrying the emotional weight of their empathy.

- **CBD for Dream Enhancement**: While research on CBD's effect on dreams is still evolving, some Pisceans report that moderate CBD consumption before bed can lead to more vivid or meaningful dreams, aligning with their deep connection to the dream world.

**Tips: Hemp Teas for Bedtime Rituals to Promote Restful Sleep and Vivid Dreams**

Incorporating hemp teas into their nighttime routine can help Pisces unwind and connect with their subconscious through restful sleep and vivid dreaming:

- **Crafting a Hemp Tea Blend**: Combining hemp flowers with herbs like mugwort, chamomile, or lavender can create a potent tea blend that promotes relaxation and enhances dream quality. Drinking this blend as part of a bedtime ritual can help Pisces slip more easily into the dream world.

- **Setting Intentions**: Before consuming their hemp tea, Pisces might find it beneficial to set intentions for their sleep or dreams, focusing their mind on healing, guidance, or creative inspiration they wish to receive from their dreamscape.

- **Journaling Post-Tea Consumption**: Keeping a dream journal beside their bed allows Pisces to record any dreams or insights upon waking. This practice can help them decipher messages from their subconscious and the universe, deepening their spiritual journey.

**Conclusion: Pisces and The Mystic's Medicine**

For Pisces, hemp serves as a mystical ally, aligning with their spiritual essence and addressing their physical sensitivities. By selecting strains that promote relaxation and enhance spiritual connectivity, and by integrating hemp into practices that support their wellbeing, such as foot care and dreamwork, Pisces can navigate both their inner and outer worlds with greater ease. Hemp teas, in particular, offer a soothing ritual that prepares them for a night of deep, restorative sleep and vivid dreams, bridging the gap between the conscious and the unconscious. In the mystic medicine of hemp, Pisces finds not just a balm for the body and mind, but a sacred elixir that nourishes their soul, guiding them closer to the universal truths they seek.

If you want to see some amazing products, please visit my Virtual Dispensary: https://shift.store/sg1fan23477/retail

## Conclusion: Weaving the Cosmic with the Cannabis

As our journey through "Zodiacal Roots: The Astrological Soul of Hemp" reaches its zenith, we reflect on the intricate tapestry woven between the celestial and the cannabis, between our cosmic blueprint and the healing virtues of hemp. This exploration has not only illuminated the unique resonances each zodiac sign shares with hemp but also underscored the profound potential for integrating this ancient plant into our lives for greater harmony, health, and spiritual growth. As we stand at the confluence of astrology and hemp medicine, we are invited to embrace a personalized approach to wellness, one that honors our individuality and the universal energies that guide us.

## Integrating Hemp into Daily Life through the Lens of Astrology

The journey of self-discovery and healing is deeply personal, yet it is also influenced by the stars under which we were born. Astrology offers a map of our deepest inclinations, strengths, and areas of challenge, providing insight into how we might harmonize with the natural world to foster wellbeing. Hemp, with its multifaceted benefits, emerges as a versatile ally in this quest, offering relief, renewal, and balance. By viewing our relationship with hemp through the lens of astrology, we open ourselves to a more nuanced understanding of how this plant can serve our unique needs, enhancing our physical health, emotional resilience, and spiritual connectivity.

## Encouraging a Personalized Approach to Hemp Medicine

The marriage of astrology and hemp medicine invites us to consider our astrological blueprint when choosing hemp strains, products, and practices. This personalized approach encourages us to tune into our body's signals and the cosmic influences that shape our being, selecting hemp solutions that resonate with our personal vibrational frequency. Whether it's choosing a CBD-rich strain for its calming effects on a water sign's emotional waves, incorporating hemp seeds into the diet of an earth sign seeking physical fortitude, or selecting sativa strains to inspire the creative fire of an air sign, this tailored approach maximizes the therapeutic potential of hemp, aligning it with our cosmic constitution.

## The Future of Astrological and Cannabis Co-Evolution

As we look to the future, the co-evolution of astrology and cannabis holds promising horizons for wellness and understanding. This alliance beckons a new era of holistic health, where the wisdom of the stars and the healing power of the earth are harmonized to guide individuals toward balance and wholeness. With the continued exploration of both fields, enriched by scientific advancements and a deepening collective consciousness, we are poised to uncover even more profound connections between our astrological makeup and the botanical world. This evolving synergy has the potential to revolutionize not only how we approach personal wellness but also how we understand the interplay between the cosmic and the terrestrial, between the universe and the self.

As we integrate hemp into our daily lives, guided by the insights of astrology, we embark on a transformative journey that honors both our individuality and our interconnectedness with the cosmos. This journey is not just about alleviating physical or emotional discomfort but about realigning with our highest selves, tapping into the ancient wisdom that links the stars above to the plants that grow beneath them. In the fusion of astrological knowledge and cannabis healing, we find a holistic path to wellness, one that nurtures body, mind, and spirit in alignment with the cosmic dance of the universe.

Thus, "Zodiacal Roots: The Astrological Soul of Hemp" serves not just as a guide to integrating hemp into our lives but as an invitation to weave the cosmic with the cannabis, stepping into a more harmonious and enlightened existence.

If you want to see some amazing products, please visit my Virtual Dispensary: https://shift.store/sg1fan23477/retail

## *Further Reading and Resources*

The exploration of the symbiotic relationship between astrology and hemp in "Zodiacal Roots: The Astrological Soul of Hemp" is merely the beginning of a fascinating journey into the cosmic and the cannabis. For those eager to delve deeper into these ancient wisdoms and modern discoveries, a rich landscape of literature, digital platforms, and communities awaits. The following curated list of recommended readings, websites, and forums is designed to guide enthusiasts, practitioners, and the curious alike towards a broader understanding and appreciation of both astrology and hemp, fostering a community of informed and mindful individuals.

## Recommended Readings

**Astrology:**

- **"The Only Astrology Book You'll Ever Need" by Joanna Martine Woolfolk:** A comprehensive guide that covers all the basics of astrology, including the signs, planets, houses, and aspects, making it an indispensable resource for beginners and experienced astrologers alike.
- **"Astrology for the Soul" by Jan Spiller:** This book offers a profound exploration of the North Node, providing insights into the spiritual life lessons each sign is meant to learn.
- **"Cosmos and Psyche: Intimations of a New World View" by Richard Tarnas:** For those interested in the intersection of astrology, psychology, and history, this book offers a compelling

analysis of planetary cycles and their correlation with historical events and cultural movements.

**Hemp and Cannabis:**

- **"The Emperor Wears No Clothes" by Jack Herer:** Often regarded as the hemp bible, this book delves into the history of hemp, its myriad uses, and the politics surrounding its prohibition.
- **"CBD: A Patient's Guide to Medicinal Cannabis--Healing without the High" by Leonard Leinow and Juliana Birnbaum:** This guide provides comprehensive information on CBD, including its therapeutic properties and how to use it for various health conditions.
- **"Cannabis Pharmacy: The Practical Guide to Medical Marijuana" by Michael Backes:** A detailed resource on using cannabis for medical purposes, covering different strains, dosages, and delivery methods.

## Websites

- **Leafly** (www.leafly.com): A leading online resource for cannabis strain information, reviews, and news, with a focus on medicinal uses and user experiences.
- **Astro.com** (www.astro.com): Offers free personalized horoscopes, professional astrological reports, and articles, making it a valuable tool for those interested in exploring their astrological chart.
- **Project CBD** (www.projectcbd.org): A non-profit organization dedicated to promoting and publicizing research into the medical uses of CBD and other components of the cannabis plant.

## Forums and Online Communities

- **Reddit - r/astrology:** A vibrant community where individuals share insights, ask questions, and discuss the various aspects of astrology.
- **Reddit - r/CBD:** A forum for CBD users to share experiences, advice, and the latest research on CBD's health benefits.
- **The Cannabis Community** (www.thecannabiscommunity.org): An online platform that offers education, support, and a forum for discussion on cannabis-related topics, including medicinal use, legalization, and industry news.

## Workshops and Conferences

- **United Astrology Conference (UAC):** Considered one of the largest gatherings of astrologers in the world, UAC offers workshops, lectures, and panels on a wide range of astrological topics.
- **Cannabis Science Conference:** This conference brings together cannabis industry experts, researchers, practitioners, and advocates to discuss the latest in cannabis science, medicine, and technology.

By engaging with these resources, readers can deepen their understanding of astrology and hemp, discovering new ways to integrate these ancient and modern practices into their lives for enhanced wellness, wisdom, and connection to the cosmos. Whether through the pages of a book, the community of an online forum, or the shared space of a workshop, the journey into the cosmic and the cannabis continues to unfold, offering endless possibilities for exploration and growth.

<u>Message from the Author:</u>

I hope you enjoyed this book, I love astrology and knew there was not a book such as this out on the shelf. I love metaphysical items as well. Please check out my other books:

-Life of Government Benefits

-My life of Hell

-My life with Hydrocephalus

-Red Sky

-World Domination:Woman's rule

-World Domination:Woman's Rule 2: The War

-Life and Banishment of Apophis: book 1

-The Kidney Friendly Diet

-The Ultimate Hemp Cookbook

-Creating a Dispensary(legally)

-Cleanliness throughout life: the importance of showering from childhood to adulthood.

-Strong Roots: The Risks of Overcoddling children

-Hemp Horoscopes: Cosmic Insights and Earthly Healing

- Celestial Hemp Navigating the Zodiac: Through the Green Cosmos

-Astrological Hemp: Aligning The Stars with Earth's Ancient Herb

-The Astrological Guide to Hemp: Stars, Signs, and Sacred Leaves

-Green Growth: Innovative Marketing Strategies for your Hemp Products and Dispensary

-Cosmic Cannabis

-Astrological Munchies

-Henry The Hemp

Check out my Virtual dispensary for all your hemp needs: https://shift.store/sg1fan23477/retail

If you want solar for your home go here: https://www.harborsolar.live/apophisenterprises/

**Instagrams: @apophis_enterprises, @hempkingdom2024, @apophisbookemporium, @apophisfashion, @apophisscardshop**

**Twitter: @apophisenterpr1, Tiktok:@apophisenterprise**

**Youtube: @sg1fan23477Top of Form**

**Podcast: Apophis Chat Zone: https://open.spotify.com/show/5zXbrCLEV2xzCp8ybrfHsk?si=fb4d4fdbdce44dec**

**Newsletter: https://apophiss-newsletter-27c897.beehiiv.com/**

www.ingramcontent.com/pod-product-compliance
Lightning Source LLC
Chambersburg PA
CBHW072127150726
47999CB00005B/2169